A Plea For Peace In A War Torn World: Poems For Calm, Wisdom And Sense

Written by

D. Brewer

Copyright

'A Plea For Peace In A War Torn World: Poems For Calm, Wisdom And Sense'

First published in August 2022 by D. Brewer

Printed and bound by Lulu Press

Distributed by Lulu Press

Poems

What is war?

What provokes war?

He said the words

Wish

Wish upon the brightest star

For kindness, love and peace

Send your wish away so far

That war and hatred cease

Kindness is the engine

Love, the fuel it needs

Peace, the goal you're searching

Your wish will sow the seeds

Allow your wish to spread and grow

Give it wings to fly

Nowhere can this wish not go

Across a troubled sky

Imagine if your wish came true

I'm sure you will agree

An age of mankind, calm and new

How peaceful it would be

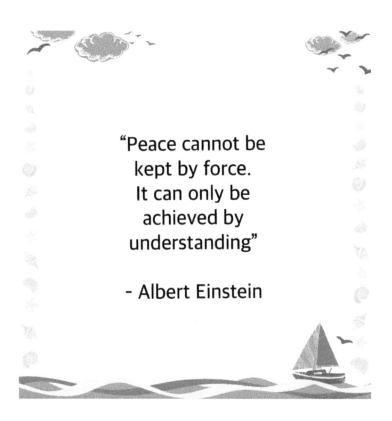

"Peace cannot be
kept by force.
It can only be
achieved by
understanding"

- Albert Einstein

Language

Imagine there's a language

That has no word for war

A language with no understanding

Of a need for law

Consider how a life would be

Without the verb, 'to fight'

It's hard to see but try

Imagine this with all your might

Intolerance, hostility

No concepts to be found

Conflict, battle, bloodshed

No words that have this sound

Anger, persecution

Cruel, unjust, unfair

These words would not exists

If only people learnt to share

The dictionary would not have

A word for any crime

Animosity would have

No place within this time

Violence and resentment

Live not within this realm

Society not guided

With base greed high at its helm

Love and peace would be

The only words to understand

Tolerance and kindness

Would rest in each human hand

Calm, sincere affection

For each soul in this domain

A language for a place

Where only love and peace would reign

How did these words access

Our languages across the Earth?

Shattering the innocence

Of cries of babes from birth

Penetrating sounds

That tell of argument and hate

Noises that our fractured minds

Found sadly to create

Are we too late to change

Our language, words to rearrange?

Our children must acknowledge

The necessity for change

Only then the human race

Will finally awake

And stop the languages of hate

For all our human sake

"Peace begins with
a smile"

- Mother Teresa

Listen, tell, what do you hear?

Listen, tell, what do you hear?
Is calm and peace with you?
The birds that sing sweet serenades
To bid the night adieu

The sea will rinse the sand again
With unrelenting tide
And gently whisper 'settle down
And rest here by my side'

The breeze will waft amid the grasses
Trees will tell their tale
Of blossom, leaf and fall 'til winter
Will their time curtail

The darkest night will disappear

The early morning sun

Will gently softly shine until

The day is good and done

So listen, tell, what do you hear?

Say, can you hear it too?

The birds, the sea, the trees, they tell

Of calm and peace with you.

"When the power
of love
overcomes the
love of power
the world will
know peace"

- Jimi Hendrix

Words

Words have so much power

Why don't people understand

How much their words affect the world

In which they have a hand?

A word can make the difference

Between war and lasting peace

A careful chosen dialogue

That can a gunfire cease

Persuasive words have power

To make leaders out of fools

Encouraging the foolish

With their ridiculous rules

The ignorant will follow

Any cause without due thought

Fake words will draw them in

To believe anything, their caught

Religious people pray aloud

With words from strong belief

To some they will bring comfort

To some they bring relief

Be careful of the danger

Words can indoctrinate

Planting seeds of anger

Promoting war and hate

Tender words of caring

Can soften any heart

Between two passing strangers

A love affair can start

Scientists use clever words

To theorise a plan

Then experiment to prove more

In the advancement of man

Harsh words will hurt a child

Destroy their hope and trust

Undermine their feelings

And turn their dreams to dust

But give a child kind words

What confidence will draw!

That child takes life on proudly

Their talents brightly soar

Wise words can change an outlook

Display a point of view

Create an understanding

Between all of them and you

So choose your words with care

Make them kind and wise and true

For they design reaction

In how people think of you

"There never was a good war,
or a bad peace"

- Benjamin Franklin

How sweet

How sweet the sun sets o'er the sea

With amber flames to comfort me

When finally the dark has won

Let night bring peace to everyone

Borders

What is a border?

Explain it to me

A demarcation

Of territory?

Inked on a parchment

Ingrained on a chart

Colour distinguishing

Countries apart

Is a border defined

By creed or religion?

By faith or belief?

By affiliation?

By national agreement?

By viewpoints or chance?

By ideological

Popular stance?

By wealth and finances?

Poverty and fear?

By resources so scarce

That none will come near?

By cultural difference?

By colour or race?

Why do we seek to have

Separate space?

Indeed, how is a border

Created at all?

How does it start

From where does it fall?

This place that keeps nations

So segregated

Maintaining identity

So Isolated

Is it a place where

They choose to agree

That differences cannot

Be settled for free?

Do borders define

Where our tolerance fails

Where cultures are fenced

And clemency pales?

Marked in geography

Settled in war

A border emerges

Controls at the door

And governments claim

Their historical right

To lands and their riches

To this end they fight

But who has the right

To inherit the world?

It's four billion years of

It's history unfurled?

Its laughable when

You consider the fraction

Of time that we've lived here

With failed interaction

Our time here is measured

'A blink of the eye'

But we've blighted it's sight

And it's started to cry

To a history of land

No man can lay claim

Yet with arrogant violence

They do all the same

And governments defend

Their borders so tightly

That bloodshed is spilt

And considered so rightly

The free are defending

Their rights from aggressors

And young lives are lost

To forbidding oppressors

And war never ends

Until new lines are drawn

New borders to fence in

A land ripped and torn

Where people have suffered

The young and the old

The men and the women

The blameless and bold

Consider the birds

It's very bizarre

They don't carry passports

But they travel far

They migrate for winter

No questioning right

No self-imposed ring fence

No impeded flight

Across human borders

And divided lands

Oceans split up

And the partitioned sands

While trees observe conflicts

Remaining unmoved

If only they showed us

How they disapproved

For centuries relentless

Through peace and through war

They shed leaves in winter

And summer grow more

They stand tall and mocking

How stupid we be

They're outliving us

The resilient tree

I really don't know

The answers I seek

We've started these borders

And now we are weak

The nature of humans

That sad honest truth

The condition we live with

Distilled In our youth

The need to control

But feel free all the same

To maintain our status

And not accept blame

Began when the very

First border was set

Who knows where it was?

Or why it was kept?

But that was the start

Of our human divides

Intolerance emerged

And humans took sides

And when sides are taken

The quarrels begin

Settled only by ceasefires

And borders within

And now we have borders

There'll never be rest

With contrasting doctrines

And lands to contest

There is no one answer

The damage is done

And humans do not even

Know what they've done

So I pray for our souls

And I pray for our sins

And I pray that a worldwide

Coalition begins

And I pray that we learn

How to peacefully live

For that is the only

Answer I give

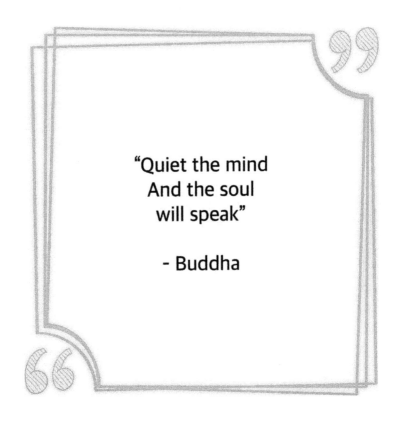

"Quiet the mind
And the soul
will speak"

- Buddha

I am the beach

I am the beach I lie on

I am the sand I feel

I am the sun that gently

Melts my soul so it can heal

I am the sea I swim in

I am the wave's caress

Of cooling salty waters

That warm me nonetheless

I am the breeze that's blowing

So gently on my skin

Reminds me that I'm living

And soothes my soul within

It's here my troubles melt away

My stresses are unwound

As here I lie in paradise

Upon this glorious ground

I am the earth around me

I am the sky above

Sublime with peace from heaven

My soul is healed with love

"If you want to make peace
with your enemy
you have to work with
your enemy.
Then he becomes
your partner"

- Nelson Mandela

Sun and Moon

I dare you to look

At the sun high above

Shining with warmth

Beaming with love

Then wait for the night

And look at the moon

Arisen in darkness

And gone all too soon

Humbly the moon

Gives the gentlest of light

Across a fair land

In the stillness of night

Then silently setting

The moon will descend

And take with her darkness

Night at an end

And just as before

The sun takes her place

Raising the morning

With promise and grace

But what is the point

Of this endless parade?

To rise in the morning

Then settle and fade?

This pattern repeating

For billions of years

Paying no heed

To our thoughts or our tears?

I dared you to look

Did you see? Did you try?

Their majesties lighting

An infinite sky?

While we toil in our world

With our quarrels and fights

With our fierce disagreements

And debatable rights

The moon still she rises

The sun will still shine

Forever in harmony

Always on time

And here down on Earth

While we battle our foes

Defending our borders

Creating our woes

How insignificant

How petty and small

To the sun and the moon

We don't matter at all

So the sun and the moon

Will both rise and descend

But the humans will die

Because that is our end

I know it is harsh

And I know it is true

For we're not immortal

Not me, and not you.

So while we exist

In this limited time

Why do we fill it

With fighting and crime?

So end to intolerance

End to the pain

End to disharmony

End to disdain

For the sun and the moon

Will not care when we die

So we must live together

We must surely try!

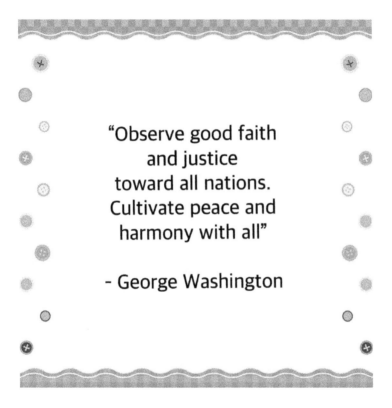

"Observe good faith
and justice
toward all nations.
Cultivate peace and
harmony with all"

- George Washington

What does peace look like?

What does peace look like to you?
Is it sky that's bright and blue?

Is it sea that's calm and deep?
Or waking from a long deep sleep?

Is it sun that's bold and bright?
Or is it moon that lights the night?

Is it blossom on the trees?
Or the gentle wafting breeze?

While I write these simple rhymes
I ponder over peaceful times

What if sky had planes of war
That through the broken sky they tore?

And what if sea had battle ships

And cries from drowning dead mens lips?

And what if when you tried to sleep

You heard the grieving mothers weep?

What if sun was blotted out

By clouds of smoke from homes bombed out?

And what of moon if smoke rose high

It darkened more the darkest sky?

If bullets and bombs struck down the trees

And no one noticed the wafting breeze?

Then what would peace look like to you?

A distant dream that might come true?

A hint of hope within your heart?

A glint of light when smoke clouds part?

A helping hand to heal the pain?

A simple smile when words are vain?

This hope for peace is in our hands

While war breaks out in distant lands

Can it come true, this dream we hold?

Or to the devil are we sold?

Within us all we have a choice

The good Lord gave us each a voice

So stand up tall and say 'no more

No to bullets, bombs and war'

The hope we have, the dreams we share

The glint of light, the peace is there

It's in our reach, just look and see

And pray for a world that's calm and free

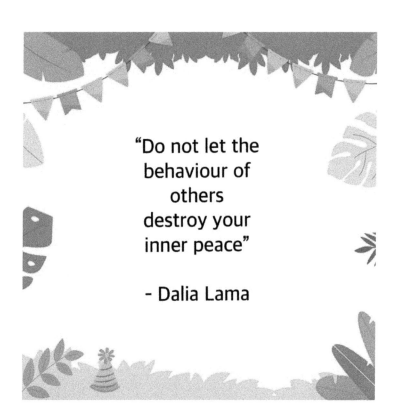

"Do not let the
behaviour of
others
destroy your
inner peace"

- Dalia Lama

Fate

The universe watches

And Fate shakes his head

Has love and compassion

Become old and dead?

Have humans forgotten

How precious their lives?

How delicate the soul

In each human survives?

Where is the tolerance?

Where is respect?

Was it extinguished?

Did it defect?

The gift they were given

Was grace and freewill

And yet they're still fighting

And yet still they kill

Where is the wisdom

And kindness of heart

That each baby holds

with each journey they start?

His head shaking still

Fate falls to his knees

With terror and fear

In the future he sees

He'd been so mistaken

To trust us with life

How could he know

It would cause so much strife

Why did he give us

A chance to know choice?

Gifted with wisdom

And lyrical voice

This wisdom so deep

And so unwisely used

This voice once so lyrical

Now badly abused

It can't be undone

It cannot be unsaid

The universe watches

While Fate shakes his head

But freewill he's given

So Fate must observe

As the humans create

Their own fate they deserve

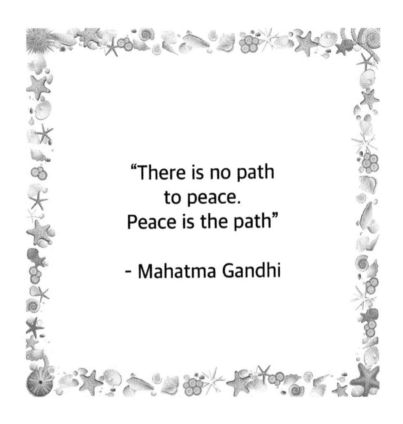

"There is no path
to peace.
Peace is the path"

- Mahatma Gandhi

Do you ever wonder?

Do you ever wonder

If an alien has passed by?

They've never ever stopped here

I really wonder why?

Imagine if an alien ship

Could reach our galaxy

And travel to our solar system

What d'you think he'd see?...

He saw an orb of light so bright

A diamond set within a ring

And precious jewels around the orb

It drew the alien in

Just one bright jewel of turquoise blue

And just a hint of green

Had caught the alien's wondering eye

His eyesight was so keen

And so he moved his rocket ship

And hid behind the moon

And hoped that he would see the sun

Rise on the Earth quite soon

But as this bright blue jewel began

To glitter in the light

The alien saw how much the Earth

Was deep in so much plight

These tiny creatures crawled along

Destroying all the planet

This can't be right, the dismayed alien thought

It can't be surely, can it?

Those lucky humans living on this

Rock of paradise

Were fighting and depleting

All the gifts for human life

The alien stayed a little while

And then, distraught, he left

He did not want to meet this world

That soon would be bereft

...I asked at the beginning

If an alien passed by

They never ever stopped here

And I really wondered why

Well now I know the answer

They've seen what humans do

And they're keeping far away from us

Well, I would too, wouldn't you?

"Education breeds
confidence.
Confidence
breeds hope.
Hope breeds peace."

- Confucius

Why?

Why would anyone

Want to savage

A snowdrop, small and quaint?

Their early hope

Of fresh new starts

Innocence incarnate

And why would anyone

Want to damage

A dancing daffodil?

That waves in wind

And smiles in sun

Beyond my window sill

And why would anyone

Choose to taint

A tulip bright and tall?

With colours fine

It flirts with Spring

And hurts no one at all

Petals open

Blossoms pop

And decorate the trees

But Mother Nature

Sighs and prays

Bending on her knees

Her work divine

Miraculous

Yet unappreciated

For still men hurt

The graceful Earth

That she freely created

The daffodil

The tulip

The snowdrop pure and white

Why would any

Man on Earth

Cause such beauty, blight?

For the daffodils

The tulips and

The snowdrops have more worth

They're metaphors

Of God's great plan

For all good men on Earth

Fresh and new

Smiling bright

With innocence they wave

Free to grow

And free to live

And nothing more they crave

Why can't all men

On Earth embrace

This plan for love and peace

No war, no fear

No greed, no hate

All worldwide conflict cease

So recognise

The finest grace

That Mother Nature grants us

And choose to live

In lasting peace

Within God's loving ethos

Then, hope renewed

Mother Nature

From her knees will raise

And men will show

Respect and awe

Bound tight with thanks and praise

"If we don't end war,
war will end us"

- H. G. Wells

Have you ever noticed?

Have you ever noticed the people in charge

Have oodles of money and wealth?

Employing accountants with black shiny shoes

Who manage their money with stealth

And big corporations are making a profit

So vast, it waters the eye

While ordinary people are working so hard

And yet they are just scraping by

Now don't get me wrong, I don't have a problem

With people who earn lots of money

I just think the chasm between rich and poor

Is increasingly gaping – how funny!

Not funny ha-ha, my tone is sarcastic

It's really not funny at all

For laughing at such an absurd situation

Would certainly make me a fool

So what is the answer? I really don't know

The poor will go on getting poor

While the rich that we work for cream off all the profits

And tell us that there is no more

The result always ends up with civil unrest

As the poor try to make themselves heard

And the ensuing protests and strikes will begin

As they march on to help spread their word

To try to placate them they're offered a pay-rise

But really, it's just not enough

They return back to work for the big corporations

and life continues to be tough

And so it goes on, this circular treadmill

And no-one can seem to escape

So the rich still get richer, exploiting the poor

And the chasm continues to gape

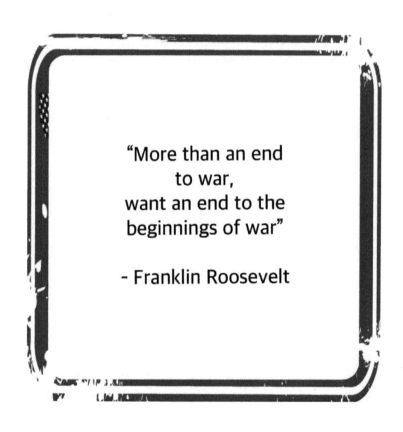

"More than an end
to war,
want an end to the
beginnings of war"

- Franklin Roosevelt

A sweet young girl

A sweet young girl is blinded

As shrapnel hits her eyes

And clouds in motion drift across

The sulking sullen skies

A young man, still a boy at heart

Lies bleeding, close to death

And birds still choose to migrate south

As he takes his final breath

A child is bewildered

His home destroyed and gone

And still the sun sets in the West

And still the hours tick on

A mother's heart is broken

Her son is killed in war

And still the cooling waters

Of the sea wash on the shore

You see, time will slow for no one

And Earth will always turn

Despite how much men harm her

When will they ever learn?

And Mother Earth is crying

As death creeps on the land

But still God holds a place for those

Who choose to hold his hand

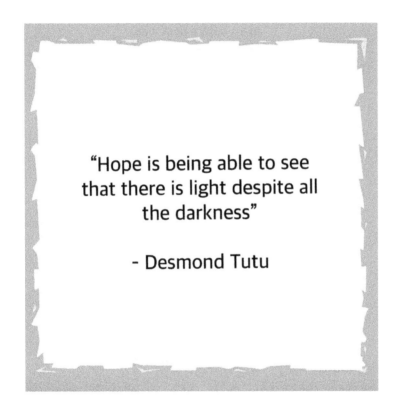

"Hope is being able to see
that there is light despite all
the darkness"

- Desmond Tutu

Where does peace start?

Where does peace start
In an outbreak of war
How d'you return
To the calm of before?

When once was the sounds
Of the birds on the breeze
And the whistle of wind
Through the leaf-laden trees

Now drowning in gunfire
And bombing and violence
And the droning of doom
From the strepitous sirens

Where once was the laughter

Of small children playing

And the murmurs of followers

Peacefully praying

Lay empty the places

Of safety and prayer

The schools and the churches

There's nobody there

Now terrified children

In bunkers reside

Clinging with parents

Together they hide

Too scared to go out

Emotionally scarred

Life for these people

Should not be this hard

So I'm asking again

In all of this turmoil

Where does peace start

On this battle trod soil

See, there must be hope

Or all will be lost

The sanity of these

Poor people the cost

And hope is a light

That never goes out

Always enduring

And lasting throughout

No matter how terrified

No matter how scared

The flickering light

Will always be there

The light of the hope

That will guide us to peace

Will eventually win

And the turmoil will cease

But where is this light

When it's difficult to see

It's inside the centre of

Both you and me

So back to my question

Where does peace start

The answer I seek is

It starts in your heart

"Once you
choose hope,
anything's possible"

- Christopher
Reeve

The war carries on

All that I want

Is some fresh food to eat

And clothes my back

And shoes on my feet

But the war carries on

In some far distant land

As a governing regime

Is making a stand

And all that I need

Is a space that is mine

Not too hot, not too cold

Simple shelter is fine

But the fighting goes on

As diplomacy failed

Troops are deployed

And war ships are sailed

I also need water

If I'm to survive

To drink and to wash

Just to keep me alive

But the fighters still torment

The poor battered town

And the once happy houses

Have all fallen down

There's not really much

That our fleeting lives need

When you take out the ambitious

Ignoble greed

But the forces that rule us

Do not comprehend

The needs of the people

They say they defend

Do they listen or hear

Or consult us at all?

Did we get any choice

When they made this mad call?

All that we want

Is some fresh food to eat

Not government sponsored

Lies and deceit

And all that we need

Is water to drink

Not media telling us

What we should think

So a space that is mine

Is all that I crave

And in it my sanity

I'll surely save

And there I believe

In simplicity find

The pathway to tread

Just to have peace of mind

"Hope is the thing with feathers

That perches in the soul

And sings the tunes without the words

And never stops at all"

-    Emily Dickinson

Ok, here's a new angle

Ok, here's a new angle

If you haven't yet heard

My thoughts as I'm speaking

In this written word

If you've not paid attention

Or read through the pages

Or misunderstood my

Rhetorical rages

See, people get sick

And children get ill

With bugs and those viruses

No one can kill

The blind still can't see

The frail still can't walk

And the mentally ill

Still need somewhere to talk

The tumours still grow

The chest pains still ache

The cancers still spread

And the bones will still break

But war is declared

And battles begin

And the truth is that really

No one will win

The poorly stay poorly

The illness remains

The war takes no notice

Of health needs and pains

There's simply no logic

In battle and fight

It's old and barbaric

In civilised sight

We should have evolved

We are better than this

But instead we descend

In a warring abyss

This evil within us

Should not be set free

Yet I fear that it has

When I see what I see

The sick are still poorly

The children still ill

The blind still can't see

And they've no hope at all

The frail still can't walk

And there's no one to tend

They've all gone to fight wars

With no certain end

So I ask what's the point

To make sick people worse?

A war is a devil's-made

Sick evil curse

"If you cannot find
peace within
yourself,
you will never find
it anywhere else"

- Marvin Gaye

Angels

The coffins lined up one by one

No one there could go

Just one priest to bless them

Only he could know

Families left devastated

None could say goodbye

Silence greeted death

As there was no one there to cry

And as the priest released them

The Angels did commune

The dead were not alone that day

Though they'd moved on too soon

Only he did witness

The miracle that day

The gathering of Angels

To guide the dead their way

Accompanied by chorus

Of pure angelic song

The arms of God himself opened

And welcomed them all home

"You will never
find peace of mind
until you listen to
your heart"

- George Michael

What is war?

What is war?

What does it mean?

A broken dialogue?

A battle machine?

A young teenage soldier

A weary platoon

A dying civilian

Gone far too soon

Calamitous crossfires

Bullets in flight

Rockets and missiles

Targets in sight

Homes are destroyed

Fires are burning

Death opens gates for the

Evil emerging

And once it is open

This gargantuan gate

Momentum increases

Emotional hate

It spreads as it grows

Covering lands

With powers of darkness

In evil-led hands

It benefits only

The creatures of power

Hungry for more precious

Land to devour

And vast corporations

Make profits from arms

That they sell to the creatures

For grossly high sums

So the rich get more money

As they profit from wars

And the people are paying

The price for their cause

And the creatures are laughing

In ivory towers

Drunk on the wealth gained

From evil-led powers

It cannot continue

But I surely know not

How to end this charade

How this evil must stop

A tragedy leaving

The people bereft

From death and destruction

They have nothing left

So I ask again

What is a war?

A tragic event

That should happen no more

"Freedom
from desire
leads to
inner peace"

- Lao Tzu

What provokes war?

What provokes war?
Is it greed? Is it hate?
Dominance demanded
By one larger state?

Belief in entitlement?
Revenge for the past?
A cry for the rights
Of a downtrodden class?

It's easy to put all the
Blame in one place
To an ideological
Thought with no face

But ask yourself this

Is it that really the cause?

When you narrow it down

And you look for the source

We're all individuals

We all have a voice

We all have been blessed

With freewill and a choice

If we all wanted peace

Then war would not exist

Patience and tolerance

Would surely persist

Ways could be found

To conclude disagreements

That would not degrade

Into violent engagements

So what provokes war?

It only takes one

To start off a quarrel

That has to be won

Then others join sides

And taking their stand

The quarrel gets bigger

And soon out of hand

The others forget

They have choice to desist

To not join a side

To fight battles, resist

It takes two to quarrel

It takes more to war

And before you know it

There's violence once more

The point that I'm making

Is if we all see

That the choices we make

For them, you and me

Are choices of reason

Of tolerance and peace

Then all of the violence

And war would just cease

Can you see how easy

Agreement could be?

If we didn't take sides

And we all remained free?

Free to be happy

Freely to share

Free to compassionately

Love, help and care

Respecting each other

Accepting our past

Living an ethos

Of peace that will last

Is this just a dream?

A wish that's been caught?

A childish fantasy?

A whimsical thought?

Maybe it's just

A naive point of view

But I still wish that one day

It may just come true

"The Earth has music
for those who listen"

- Shakespeare

He said the words

He said the words

For us to hear

He said them loud and clearly

Love thy neighbour

Learn to share

Be kind and love sincerely

It's not that hard

To understand

It's not that tricky really

So love thy neighbour

Knowing that

Our own God loves us dearly

End

Lightning Source UK Ltd.
Milton Keynes UK
UKHW020851230822
407709UK00010B/768